WATERLOO HIGH SCHOOL LIBRARY
1464 iN
ATWATER

W9-AMV-823

WATERLOO HIGH SCHOOL LIBRARY
1464 INDUSTRY RD.
ATWATER, OHIO 44201

Everything You Need to Know About

SMOKING

Teenagers sometimes start to smoke because they think it will make them look "cool."

WATERLOO HIGH SCHOOL LIBRARY
1464 INDUSTRY RD.
ATWATER, OHIO 44201

• THE NEED TO KNOW LIBRARY •

Everything You Need to Know About

SMOKING

Elizabeth Keyishian

Series Editor: Evan Stark, Ph.D.

THE ROSEN PUBLISHING GROUP, INC.
NEW YORK

613.85
KEY

Published in 1989, 1993 by The Rosen Publishing Group, Inc.
29 East 21st Street, New York, New York 10010

Revised Edition 1993
Copyright © 1989, 1993 by The Rosen Publishing Group, Inc.

All rights reserved. No part of this book may be reproduced in any form without permission in writing from the publisher, except by a reviewer.

Manufactured in the United States of America.

Library of Congress Cataloging-in-Publication Data

Keyishian, Elizabeth
    Everything you need to know about smoking/Elizabeth Keyishian
    (The need to know library)
    Includes bibliographical references and index.
    Summary: Discusses the dangerous effects of smoking. Why people
start, why it's so hard to quit, and how to stop smoking.
    ISBN 0-8239-1615-4
    1. Tobacco habit—Juvenile literature. 2. Smoking—Juvenile literature.
3. Youth—Tobacco use—Juvenile literature. [1. Smoking.]
I. Title. II. Title: Smoking. III. Series.
HV5745.K48   1989
813.85—dc20   89-10256
                                             CIP
                                             AC

Contents

Introduction

When you see a billboard, a bus or subway ad, or a magazine ad for cigarettes, what do you think? What catches your eye first? Is it the picture, a photo of young, good-looking people having fun together, or a cartoon animal who dresses "cool"? Do you even *see* the white box at the bottom of the panel, the "warning label" that all packs and ads must carry?

The more we learn about the health problems smoking can cause, the harder tobacco companies try to get young people to start smoking. Once you start smoking, it's hard to quit. You can get "hooked" on smoking because tobacco smoke contains *nicotine*. Nicotine is a drug that your body becomes addicted to. Some people who have smoked for many years try over and over to stop smoking. Because they have smoked so many cigarettes a day for so long, they need help from a doctor in order to quit.

Many laws have been passed that ban smoking in public places. Many states have laws that require restaurants, for example, to provide special sections for non-smokers. The reason for laws like these is that we now know that you can suffer from smoking-related health problems even if you *don't* smoke. Being affected by the smoking of others is called *passive* smoking.

A lot of people *are* getting smarter about smoking. A survey was conducted recently to put together a picture of the "typical" American. Are you surprised that the typical American is *not* a smoker? Forty-seven percent of the people said that they had *never* smoked, and twenty-five percent said that they had quit. Only twenty-eight percent of the people said that they were smokers.

Why does smoking still appeal to some people, even though they know it causes health problems and offends many people? Do young people think smoking makes them look older, or more grown up? Do women think that smoking helps them to eat less? This book will give you some answers to questions like these.

Why are you thinking about the subject of smoking? Do you have a friend who smokes and you are curious? If you picked up this book because smoking is on your mind, the information that follows will help you decide what is right for you. It may even convince you to try to help your friend quit smoking, instead.

The first cigarette can make you feel sick.

Chapter 1

Starting to Smoke

It has been many years since the release of the U.S. Surgeon General's Report on Smoking and Lung Cancer. Since that time there have been many more studies on the health risks of smoking. We now know that smoking can harm non-smokers, too. Being around people who smoke is—as cigarette labels warn—"hazardous to your health."

Many more people are non-smokers today than in the past. One of the reasons for the change is that people know smoking is dangerous. And people know how hard it is to quit smoking once you start. Smoking is also an expensive habit. A big part of the cost of a pack of cigarettes is taxes. Taxes on cigarettes go higher and higher. But people still smoke. And new people still *start* smoking, every day.

Reasons Why

Why would people want to do something that is dangerous for them and for others? Why would they want to start something that is so hard to stop?

Some studies suggest that people start to smoke because the people around them do it. If your mother or father smokes, you are more likely to start smoking. If a sister or brother has started smoking, or a close friend, you are more likely to try it. When you admire people, you want to be like them. If you love or admire people who smoke, it is more likely you will start to smoke.

Some young people start smoking because they think it makes them look grown-up. They think that imitating grown-ups is the same as being an adult. Young people smoke because they see older people smoke and want to be treated as an adult, too. It is against the law for TV to have ads for cigarettes, but movies often show people smoking. And movies are shown on TV, too. So young people see famous, glamorous people smoking, and then think that smoking is okay. Think about movies you have seen. Do they show tough guys or beautiful young women smoking cigarettes? Think what those movies may "say" to you.

Researchers say that most people start smoking because their family or friends smoke.

Lung disease is often a result of smoking over a period of time.

Many young people smoke because their friends do. Young people act alike because they feel better being part of a group than having to be alone. Feeling that you should do something because others do it is called *peer pressure.* (See Chapter 4: Everybody's Doing It. But Should You?) If one person in your group starts smoking, others may try it, too. And some of you might dislike it, but be afraid to tell the others. So all of you keep smoking. And if you continue to smoke, you may find it hard to stop. It will become a habit—a bad habit.

Some young girls start to smoke because they think that smoking will help them eat less.

Cigarette smoke contains *nicotine,* which is a drug. That means you may get *addicted* to smoking, and find it very hard to stop.

Think Again

Even if you thought smoking **did** help you to stay thin, you may not be considered attractive to others. Smoking gives you bad breath. It can stain your teeth. It makes your clothes smell bad. Even your hair will smell like tobacco if you smoke a lot.

You can tell that smoking is not good for you by the way your body reacts to it. The first time you smoke it usually makes you cough. You may choke or feel dizzy. You may even feel sick enough to throw up. Cigarette smoke contains *tar.* Tar stays in your lungs even though you blow the smoke back out through your nose or mouth. Tar in your lungs can cause cancer. Smoking can also cause heart disease and other serious health problems. Even if you *do* enjoy smoking, is the pleasure worth sacrificing your health or even your life?

You should think about all of these things when someone offers you a cigarette, or talks about how "cool" it is to smoke. Don't be afraid to say no. There are no good reasons to start to smoke. People will respect you for making your own decision.

Chapter 2

The Health Risks

Maybe you already know what smoking does to your body. You've heard that smoking causes diseases. Even the warning label on the cigarette pack says how dangerous it is.

But you see a lot of healthy-looking people who smoke. They don't look as if they have cancer or heart disease. And most of the people who get sick are so much older than you.

When 40-year-old people get cancer or heart disease from smoking, they think, "I wish I had never started smoking." Of course, then it's too late.

The earlier you start smoking, the earlier you can die from a smoking-related illness.

To understand how terrible smoking is for you, look at what each cigarette contains:

○ Nicotine—a habit-forming drug.
○ Black tars that stick to the lining of your lungs and make it hard to breathe.
○ Carbon monoxide and chemicals that poison your lungs.

Every drag on a cigarette leaves those things in your lungs.

Nicotine speeds up your heart. It makes your nerves shaky. In large doses, it is poisonous. You quickly become addicted to it.

The tars coat the inside of your lungs and make it hard to breathe. Your heart has to work harder. It is not getting enough oxygen from your stuffed-up lungs.

Carbon monoxide prevents oxygen from getting to your heart. That can cause heart disease.

How does smoking affect your body? Your body is like a sensitive machine. Its parts work together to keep you healthy. When you smoke, you damage many parts of the machine. That makes it break down. Soon, the machine stops working.

You breathe all day long. We take about 600 million breaths during our lifetime. When was the last time you said: "Wow. I'm breathing."

Smoking cuts down lung power. It becomes difficult to breathe while running or walking.

Probably never. You have too many other things to think about. You only think about breathing when it hurts to breathe.

When you smoke, you make breathing more difficult. Try running up a flight of stairs. You might find yourself breathing very heavily and your heart racing.

There are pictures that can show you what happens to your lungs and heart when you smoke. Surgeons who operate on smokers say that the lungs are black from tar.

Lungs bring oxygen into the body and pump carbon dioxide out. The lungs are made of tubes called *bronchi*. The tubes lead into tiny balloon-like sacs. In the tubes, tiny hairs (called *cilia*) brush mucus out of the airways.

Nicotine—the drug in the tobacco—paralyzes your cilia. The cilia can't push the mucus out of the way. Your airways get clogged. Tars and chemicals settle in the airways and the cilia die. The smoker has to cough to get the mucus out of the lungs. That's "smoker's cough." It sounds like someone choking and wheezing.

The bronchi (those tubes in your lungs) get sore with all that coughing. The smoker then develops "chronic bronchitis." It becomes more painful and difficult to breathe.

People with bronchitis often develop *emphysema,* a disease that makes it hard to breathe. Many of them have to use a wheelchair. Simple movements—like walking and breathing—are like climbing Mount Everest. Some people with emphysema are easy to spot. They have to wheel around a little cart of oxygen wherever they go.

People who smoke for a long time may also get cancer. The chemicals and tars in cigarettes make the body cells grow out of control. They form lumps—tumors—in the lungs. The cancerous lumps block breathing.

Smoking is also very hard on the heart. The lungs, heart, and blood vessels all work together. When you smoke, you breathe in nicotine and carbon monoxide. The nicotine and carbon monoxide make the blood vessels smaller. Less oxygen gets to the heart, so the heart has to work harder. Heart disease causes heart attacks.

There is *one* piece of good news. As soon as you stop smoking, your body begins to repair itself. The sooner you stop smoking, the less damage you'll do to your body.

Special Health Risks for Women

Smoking is dangerous for everybody. But there are special health risks for women.

Girls aged 14 to 17 are smoking more and more, even though there are health risks. That may be because of cigarette advertising. It may also be because they think that cigarettes keep weight down.

Lung cancer has replaced breast cancer as the leading killer disease of women. If you smoke and take birth control pills, you are TEN TIMES MORE LIKELY than average to have a heart attack or stroke. Smoking increases the risk of heart attack for young women more than any other factor. You don't have to be old to have a heart attack.

Remember the warning label: "Smoking by pregnant women may result in fetal injury, premature birth, and low birth weight."

Why should you worry about that now? It may not seem important to you yet. But once you start smoking, it is very, very hard to quit. When you become a mother, you may still be smoking.

Babies of mothers who smoke have twice the risk of having Sudden Infant Death syndrome. This kills babies, suddenly, in their sleep. Also, the babies of smokers have twice as many lung illnesses—like bronchitis and pneumonia.

Chapter 2: Summary

- The earlier you start smoking, the earlier you can die from it.
- Cigarettes contain nicotine, tars, carbon monoxide, chemicals. Nicotine is a habit-forming drug. Tars coat your lungs and make it difficult to breathe. Carbon monoxide is deadly for your heart.

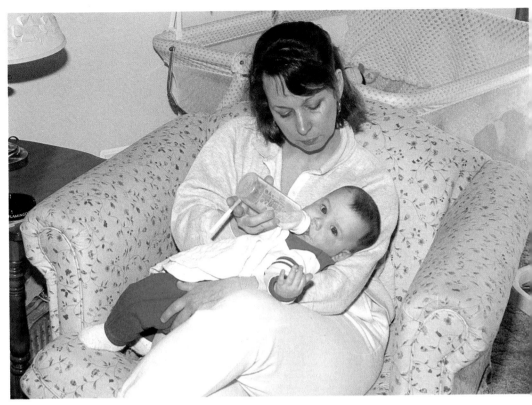

A baby's health can be affected if its mother smokes.

○ Smoking causes lung diseases: chronic bronchitis and emphysema and lung cancer.
○ Smoking causes heart disease. Smoking gives people strokes and heart attacks.
○ The sooner you stop smoking, the less damage you will do to your body. But the longer you smoke, the higher your chances of getting lung or heart diseases.
○ There are special health risks for women who smoke. Lung cancer has replaced breast cancer as the leading cause of cancer death among women.
○ Women who smoke during pregnancy endanger their babies.

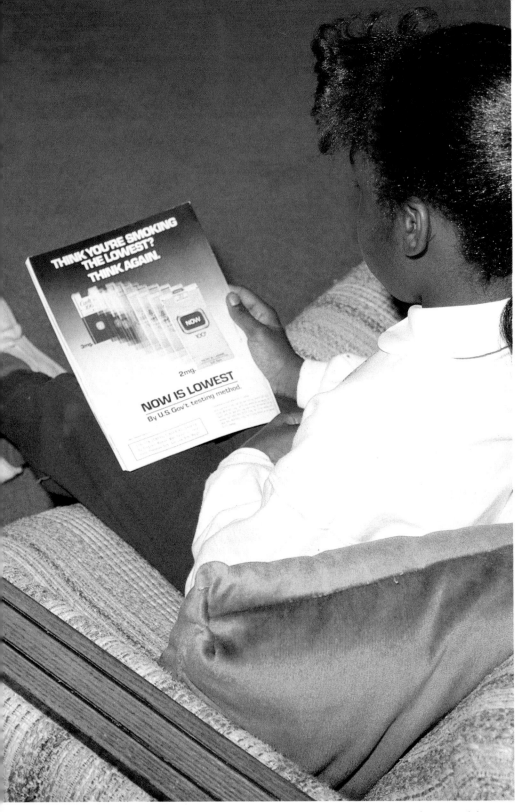

Cigarette ads always have a warning but they try to make smoking look safe and glamorous.

Chapter 3

What You See Is Not What You Get

Cigarette advertising has a hard job to do. Ads must make smoking look like something you will enjoy doing. They must make smoking look good enough to make you try it even though the same ad has a warning about smoking being harmful. The ads must have the warnings. That is the law. The law was passed so that everyone would know the dangers of smoking.

Older people who smoke don't need advertising to convince them. A lot of people who smoke would stop if they could, but they are "hooked." Smoking is a habit. You get used to it, and you miss it if you try to stop. And many people get addicted to the nicotine in tobacco smoke. Their bodies need it and they feel sick, or very nervous, if they do not smoke.

Older people who do not smoke will probably not be convinced by ads that smoking is a good thing. But tobacco companies and advertising executives think that they can make smoking look good to young people. That's why a lot of cigarette advertising is aimed at young people.

Cigarette ads show carefree couples having a good time. They make it look as if you will have fun because you smoke. They make you think that smoking will make you popular. That kind of advertising suggestion is called *association*. Linking something pleasant with a product makes people want to try the product.

Often the ads show couples outdoors together, or even show people playing sports. In real life, people who smoke a lot can have trouble breathing. Smoking makes it hard to play active sports. If you are on a team, the coach will tell you not to smoke.

Ads show people who are healthy, with glowing skin and brilliant white teeth. In truth, smoking stains your teeth. It makes your skin dull. It makes your hair smell bad.

Some people think that cigarette advertising should not be allowed. It is not allowed on TV. In the city of New York, cigarette advertising is not allowed on buses or subways any more.

It is against the law to sell cigarettes to minors (people younger than 18). But cigarette ads seem to be directed toward younger and younger kids. One cigarette company uses a cartoon character in its ads.

Sometimes the character is shown with a group of other "cool" characters. These ads appear on billboards and in store windows. They appear in magazines that kids read. One study showed that most fourth graders could more easily identify this cartoon character than a photo of the current president of the United States.

Cigarette companies sell, or give away with the purchase of cigarettes, T-shirts, caps, lighters, and other items. These items feature the name of their brand of cigarettes. When you use these items, you are giving the company *free advertising.* You become a walking cigarette ad!

A Different Kind of Advertising

There is another side to more recent cigarette advertising. Health-related groups like the American Cancer Society and the Heart Association have ads, too. Their ads stress the dangers of smoking. At first the advertising companies tried to block these kinds of ads. They threatened not to buy space from companies that sold space to anti-smoking ads.

But the message about the dangers of smoking is very important. The cigarette companies spend over a billion dollars a year to convince people that smoking is not bad for them. Now there is something being done to let people know the truth about smoking.

Friends will respect your wish not to smoke.

Chapter 4

Everybody's Doing It. But Should You?

Most people start smoking because their friends smoke. A friend tells you to try smoking. And its easier to say yes than no.

But what if you don't want to smoke? Or maybe you haven't made up your mind. You don't want to be pushed into deciding. The decision to smoke or not to smoke should be *your* decision. But what do you say to friends who want you to be like them—who want you to smoke?

Picture yourself in the following scene. This is how you might deal with three friends who are pressuring you to smoke:

You are outside a video arcade with Tina, Frank, and Billy. They want to have a cigarette before they go in. You are the only non-smoker.

Tina: You want a cigarette?

You: No, thanks.

Frank: Hey, how come you're not smoking?

Billy: You trying to save your lungs for the Olympics?

You: I don't know if I want to smoke.

Tina: Well, try one. How are you going to decide if you don't try one?

Billy: Here, I'll even light one for you. (He takes a cigarette from Tina's pack.)

You: Don't waste your breath, Billy. I'm not ready to try one.

Frank: Practically everybody smokes. What are you so worried about? Afraid that your mom will find out?

Tina: You're chicken.

You: If I was chicken, I'd have feathers. Look, I don't want to spend money on cigarettes. Besides, they don't call them "cancer sticks" for nothing.

Billy: You believe that crap? Look at me. Do I look like I have cancer?

Tina: No, but you still look sick.

Billy: Funny. Very funny.

Frank: When I smoke, it gives me a little rush— a little high. You should try it. If you don't like it, you can quit.

You: Yeah, well, I figure I can start any time. Quitting's a little tougher, I hear.

Tina: What is your problem? You sound so high and mighty.

Cigarettes are expensive. Saving some extra money can be a good reason not to smoke.

You: Look, you can smoke if you want to. It's fine. It's your business. If that's what you want, do it. But I think you should respect my right *not* to smoke, too.

Frank: Okay, I just thought you might want to try something new.

You (grinning): Okay, I'll try something new. I'll beat Billy's high score on Space Invaders.

Billy: No way.

You: C'mon, Billy.

Tina: *This* should be fun to see.

You: Hey, this might be my lucky day.

You might be in a situation like this sometime. You can be firm about not smoking without getting angry. Your friends will respect you for holding your ground.

They won't show it then. They may be really pushy or act mad. But they will admire you for making your own choice.

Standing up for yourself will make *you* feel better too. You have made your own decision. That is a big step toward becoming an adult.

And, because you've firmly told your friends how you feel, they probably won't push you to smoke again.

Chapter 4: Summary

○ Many people start smoking because their friends smoke. Sometimes friends may even pressure you to start.

○ Be firm and direct with your friends. Explain your position on smoking. Don't get angry. Make jokes.

○ Your friends will respect you for standing up for yourself.

Standing up for yourself will make *you* feel better too. You have made your own decision.

Chapter 5

Addiction to Nicotine

Once you start smoking, it's *very hard* to quit. Why? Your body is addicted to a drug—nicotine. A report from the Surgeon General says that nicotine is an addictive drug. Being addicted means that your body urgently needs the drug.

Nicotine is also a poison. Chemical companies use nicotine to make a very powerful insecticide. In other words, nicotine is used as a bug killer! No person inhales that much nicotine, but even small amounts do terrible things.

You can become addicted to nicotine very quickly. Some people say that they are not really addicted to cigarettes. But they don't realize that they are hooked on nicotine.

A person addicted to cigarettes needs to light up first thing in the morning.

Smoking can give you a quick spurt of energy, but it does not last long.

When the nicotine level in the bloodstream gets low, the body signals the mind: "Smoke a cigarette. I need nicotine."

As soon as the smoker lights up, the nicotine is drawn into the lungs. It is quickly absorbed into the blood. The body's nicotine craving is satisfied—for a while.

Nicotine is a sneaky drug. When you first start smoking you find that smoking gives you a little burst of energy. That's the nicotine speeding up your heart.

But after a while you notice that you feel tired between cigarettes. That happens when the nicotine level gets low. The tired feeling is your body's way of telling you that it wants nicotine.

The smoker is like a prisoner on a seesaw. When you're "down" on the seesaw, your body feels "withdrawal." That's what makes you feel tired and sluggish. Your body wants its dose of nicotine.

So you smoke a cigarette.

Now you're "up" on the seesaw. Nicotine speeds up the heart. It gives you a "rush." It stimulates the *adrenal* gland. That's the gland that makes *adrenaline*—the stuff that pumps through your veins when you're excited or nervous.

That's what creates that seesaw feeling. The nicotine gives you a rush. But when the nicotine level goes down, you feel the withdrawal symptoms. So, although some people smoke to wake themselves up, they end up being more tired.

Chapter 5: Summary

○ When you smoke, your body becomes addicted to nicotine.

○ It is very easy to become addicted to nicotine.

○ Nicotine addiction makes you feel like a prisoner on a seesaw.

Many people think that smoking helps them to eat less.

Chapter 6

Why Smoking Is Hard to Give Up

The addiction to nicotine is one BIG reason why it's hard to quit smoking. But it's not the *only* reason. If you've been smoking for a while, smoking becomes a habit.

Why is smoking so hard to give up? These four stories might give you an idea:

Jennifer has been a smoker for two years. She's afraid to quit because she thinks that she'll gain weight. She smokes cigarettes when she's hungry because that takes away her appetite. And smoking gives her something to do with her hands.

Jennifer's boyfriend is very athletic. He likes to go hiking and play tennis. Jennifer hasn't been able to

*keep up with him. She often feels out of breath even
after a few minutes. She knows it's because she
smokes. But she's afraid to quit. She heard that people
put on a lot of weight when they quit.*

Jennifer smokes because she doesn't want to gain
weight. A lot of women feel that way, especially
young women. Television, movies, and magazines
make women feel that they have to be thin.

But smoking won't necessarily keep you thin.
The more you smoke, the less you exercise.
Doctors say that exercise and good eating habits
keep weight off. If Jennifer quit smoking and took
up hiking, she'd be thin *and* healthy.

*Frank smokes a cigarette after every meal and when
he's watching television. He doesn't even think about
it. Sometimes he's surprised to find a lighted cigarette
in his hand. He can't even remember lighting it.*

*One night Frank was smoking in bed. He fell asleep
with a lighted cigarette. Luckily, his little brother
smelled something burning. He walked in and found
Frank's blanket on fire. He woke Frank up,
screaming. They were able to put the fire out before it
got out of control.*

For Frank, smoking has become part of his daily
routine. A routine is something you follow without
even thinking about it—like brushing your teeth.

Before you go to bed, you brush your teeth. Going to bed is a "signal" to brush your teeth. Smokers have signals too: Frank's signals to smoke are finishing a meal or watching TV.

If you're a smoker, it's a good idea to figure out what your signals to smoke are. One man was determined to quit smoking. He found that a morning cup of coffee was his signal to smoke. He had to give up the coffee in order to give up the cigarettes!

Joanne feels awkward unless she has a cigarette in her hand. She's very shy. Smoking allows her to hide behind the smoke. Meeting people makes her really nervous, but if she has a cigarette in her hand she feels more in control.

When Joanne is in a situation where she can't smoke, she panics. She doesn't go to places where she is not allowed to smoke.

Joanne uses smoking as a crutch. She can smoke instead of talk. She hopes that smoking will help her feel relaxed.

People see Joanne in a cloud of smoke. But Joanne can't hide behind the smoke forever. She has to learn how to be herself without cigarettes.

David's parents fight a lot. David gets really stressed out when his parents fight. When they fight,

*he chain-smokes in his room for hours. He is still
smoking long after the shouting has stopped.*

*The only way he can keep calm is to smoke. After
smoking so many cigarettes, he feels sick. That takes
his mind off his parents and their fighting.*

David is under a lot of stress. Stress is something
you feel when you feel nervous or pressured. You
might be very tense because of a big test or a job
interview. Or, like David, there might be a lot of
tension at home.

All of your fears and tensions create stress. Stress
makes you feel out of balance. It makes you feel
that you have to *do* something. David smokes when
he's under stress. He smokes until he feels sick.

David's guidance counselor recommended that
David take a long bike ride every Saturday
morning. David followed the advice. It helped him
work out his feelings. It felt good to ride hard and

Smoking in bed is very dangerous.

fast. After those rides, his parents' fights did not bother him as much.

Lots of things cause stress—school, family, work. Even feeling tired can cause stress, if you have to stay awake to study or work late at your job.

Exercising is one way to reduce stress. But there are other ways. Take a walk. Take a nap. Listen to music or watch TV.

If you know a stressful situation is coming up, try to plan ahead. Give yourself a healthy way to get rid of the stress.

Smoking is not the way. It will end up *causing* stress, instead of helping it.

Chapter 6: Summary

○ Smoking is hard to give up because it's a habit.
○ Smoking is not a healthy way to keep your weight down. Many fat people smoke. Exercise is a way to be lean and healthy.
○ Smoking is something you might do without even thinking about it. Most smokers have "signals" that tell them when to light up. For example, a morning cup of coffee might be a signal to smoke.
○ Many people smoke when they are under stress. School, family, work, even feeling tired can cause stress. There are healthy ways to deal with stress: exercise, nap, listen to music, take a walk.

Sports and smoking do not mix. Most smokers do not have enough energy to enjoy exercise.

Chapter 7

Good Reasons Not to Smoke

You may have heard this expression before: "Kissing a smoker is like licking an ashtray." Smoker's breath has also been called "zoo breath." Not only does a smoker's breath stink, but so do a smoker's hair and clothing. Smoking also leaves brown or yellow marks on teeth and fingers.

You might start smoking to be "in" with a certain group. But what about being friends with people who don't smoke? Many non-smokers think that smoking is disgusting. If you're a smoker, it could *limit* your social life.

Non-smokers don't like the smell of the smoke. They also don't like the fact that your cigarette smoke could hurt them. (See Chapter 8: Involuntary Smoking.) If you start smoking, you may actually lose more friends than you gain.

Smoking can limit your job options. Some places won't hire you if you smoke! And other companies put limits on where and when you can smoke at work.

The anti-smoking laws make it illegal to smoke in certain parts of restaurants. On short airplane flights, smoking is not permitted. Soon, smoking may be banned from all public places.

If you're still not convinced, think about this: Smoking is expensive. The cost of cigarettes is going up and up. Today, an average pack costs about $1.35. If you smoke a pack a day, that's $492.75 a year. With that much money, you could buy new clothes, go to seventy movies, or even pay for part of a sunny vacation.

Other costs include dry-cleaning bills. You need to spend extra money to get the cigarette smell out of your clothes.

Smoking also limits your sense of smell. And studies have shown that smoking gives you wrinkles and makes your skin look unhealthy.

Chapter 7: Summary

○ Smokers have stinky hair, breath, and clothes. Smoker's breath has been called "zoo breath."

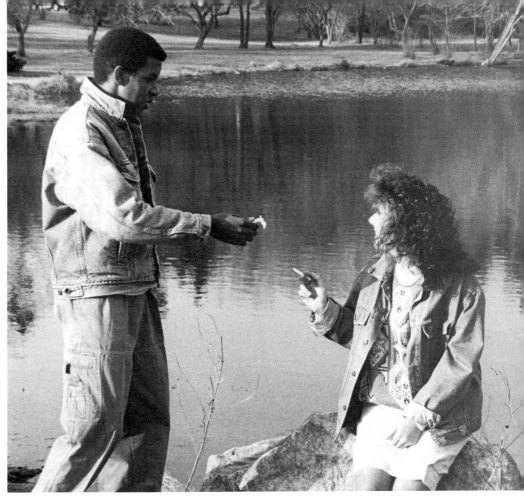

Bad breath is not romantic! Many smokers use gum or mints to cover up cigarette breath.

○ Smoking can limit your social life. Non-smokers don't want to be exposed to the health risks of smoking. Also, they don't like the stink of smoke. So non-smokers may avoid smokers.
○ Smoking can limit your job options.
○ Anti-smoking laws make it illegal to smoke in sections of restaurants and in some public places.
○ Smoking is expensive.
○ Smoking limits your sense of smell.
○ Smoking gives you wrinkles and makes your skin look unhealthy.

43

Non-smokers are affected by the smoke around them.

Chapter 8

When Others Smoke

Let's say you don't smoke. Think about riding in a car or being in a closed room with a smoker. But the smoker's burning cigarette makes it hard for *you* to breathe.

New studies have shown that this smoke—from someone else's cigarette—can be harmful to *your* health. Non-smokers are very angry about this.

Most states in the United States have a law that protects non-smokers. It is illegal in those states to smoke in many public places, like elevators and some buildings. Some states require that restaurants have two sections: one for smokers, and one for non-smokers. It is also against the law to smoke cigarettes, or tobacco in any form, on airplanes. Many workplaces have also been declared "smoke-free zones."

What are non-smokers worried about?
There are two kinds of smoke that come from a
lighted cigarette:
    1) "mainstream" smoke
    2) "sidestream" smoke

Mainstream smoke is what the smoker inhales
into his or her lungs. Think of a smoker taking a
drag in slow motion. The smoke passes through
the filter of the cigarette. The filter traps some of
the chemicals and tars. Then the smoke enters the
lungs. The lungs filter out more of the harmful
substances. Then the smoker exhales.

Sidestream smoke is the smoke that goes directly
into the air from the tip of a burning cigarette.
This smoke does not pass through a filter. It
contains a lot more carbon monoxide, tars, and
nicotine than the mainstream smoke.

Sidestream smoke is what non-smokers breathe
when they are in a room with smokers. The carbon
monoxide makes them feel tired. It gives them
headaches. Studies have shown that non-smokers
who live with smokers die younger than people
who live in smoke-free houses.

A famous television writer died of lung cancer.
He had *never* smoked. His partner had smoked
more than two packs of cigarettes every day. The
two men had worked together for over 20 years.
How do you think the surviving partner felt about
what had happened? Would you want something
like that to happen to someone you care about?

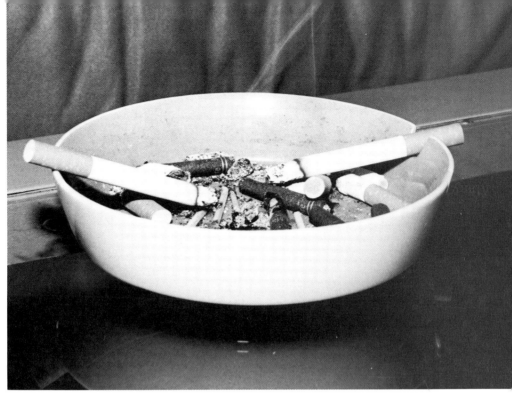

The smoke from lit cigarettes in the ashtray can be harmful.

What does all this mean? The non-smoker who lives or works with smokers can get as sick from the smoke as smokers. Is that fair?

What do you think?

Chapter 8: Summary

○ The smoke from a cigarette can harm non-smokers too.
○ Mainstream smoke is what a smoker inhales. It is filtered by the smoker's lungs. More poisonous to the non-smoker is sidestream smoke. That smoke contains all the unfiltered poisons: tars, carbon monoxide, etc.
○ The non-smoker who lives or works with smokers can also get sick from smoke.

Talking with counselors and other teens can be helpful in making a decision about not smoking.

Chapter 9

Do You WANT to Smoke? Make Your Own Decision

Now you know more about smoking. You know how it affects your body, your appearance, and your health. You know more about why people start and why it's hard to stop.

Maybe you haven't started smoking, but you're thinking about it. Choosing whether or not to smoke is an important decision. This "test" will help you. If you're already a smoker, try this test. It may change your mind about smoking.

This is the "Smoker's Decision Test." It isn't like a school test. There are no right or wrong answers. This is a way to help you get a clearer idea of what's important to you. It will help you make the decision about smoking.

Check one box for each statement.

Part One: Reasons for Smoking

	Very Important	Not Important
1. Smoking can make you feel like part of the group.	☐	☐
2. Smoking can make you feel more mature and glamorous.	☐	☐
3. If you already smoke, you'd be giving up something that makes you feel good.	☐	☐
4. Smoking relaxes you.	☐	☐
5. You don't want to admit that it was a mistake to start smoking.	☐	☐
6. Quitting might cause you to gain weight.	☐	☐
7. You don't want to face the possibility that your smoking is out of control and you can't quit.	☐	☐

Most people find it easy to use the result of this test. They can see clearly how they feel about smoking.

Look at what you have checked. Look closely at what you have checked in the "Very Important" column.

Check one box for each statement.

Part Two: Reasons for Not Smoking

	Very Important	Not Important
1. Smoking can limit your social life.	☐	☐
2. Smoking is bad for your health. It can even kill you.	☐	☐
3. It is bad for the health of others around you.	☐	☐
4. It has special health risks for women.	☐	☐
5. It can limit job opportunities.	☐	☐
6. It reduces athletic ability.	☐	☐
7. It is an expensive habit.	☐	☐
8. It makes your breath, clothes, and hair smell bad.	☐	☐

Now write out your "Very Important" reasons for smoking and your "Very Important" reasons for not smoking. Compare them side by side.

Look at your reasons. DECIDE FOR YOURSELF if you are going to start. If you have already started, decide if you are going to continue or quit. Either way, make your own decision.

Setting a date is an important part of trying to stop smoking.

Chapter 10

How to Quit Smoking

If you are a smoker, you may have tried to quit. You may have found that it's very, very hard.

Now the good news! Nearly half of all living adults who ever smoked have quit. That's *millions* of people who have quit smoking. You can too. There is no guaranteed method. You have to find what's right for you. Here are some steps to follow to help you kick the habit.

1. Don't Leave Home Without It

Make a list of all the reasons why you want to quit. (I hate the way cigarettes smell. I want clean lungs.) *You* must decide why you want to quit. Is it the cost? The complaints from your boyfriend or girlfriend about the smoke?

Write down those reasons. Keep the list with you. Every day, pull out the list and remind yourself: This is why I'm quitting.

2. Set a Date

Choose a quitting date on the calendar. Don't change it. If you know you smoke most often at school or work, choose a weekend to quit. That will make the first one or two days easier.

Some people quit "cold turkey." That means they choose a day to quit, and they quit—completely.

Other people cut down first. That means that they smoke fewer cigarettes. Then they quit.

3. Cutting Down

The cutting down period should last only three weeks. Set your quitting date for three weeks later.

Here's how to cut down:

You probably smoke a certain number of cigarette without even thinking about it. Other cigarettes, like the ones you smoke after a meal or after a test, are more important to you. At those times you really *want* a cigarette.

The trick to cutting down is to decide which cigarettes are important to you—and smoke ONLY those cigarettes.

You can plan ahead of time. Carry a cigarette pack with the exact number of cigarettes you have decided to smoke that day. It might be just three or four.

Another way to cut down is to smoke only half a cigarette at a time. Or change to a brand of cigarettes you don't like.

Still another way to cut down is to delay having a cigarette when you want one. Instead of smoking when you want to, wait ten minutes. That way, you can think it over and decide if you *really* want that cigarette. You may find that after ten minutes you don't want the cigarette anymore.

Cutting down is great. But don't fool yourself. You may think that you have things under control. You may think you can quit anytime. That's not true. Most people who cut down soon return to their original number of cigarettes.

Limit the cutting-down period to three weeks. Set your quitting date!

4. Tell Everybody You're Quitting

Tell your family and friends about your plan to quit smoking. That will make it harder for you to back out of it. It will also let others know that you might be cranky and a little hard to live with for a few days.

5. Don't Change Your Eating Habits

Don't reach for a snack every time you want a cigarette. Chew gum. Exercise. If you snack, that might make you gain weight. People use weight gain as an excuse to start smoking again.

6. Reward Yourself

Find other things to do that are fun or make you happy. An easy choice is exercise. Exercise is good because you have to use your lungs and body. That reminds you of how important clean lungs are. Also, exercise makes you feel good.

Or take up a hobby—photography, music, skateboarding.

Go to the movies, the zoo, the beach, a concert. To pay for these activities, use the money you're not spending on cigarettes!

7. DON'T GIVE UP!

If you smoke a cigarette or even an entire pack, don't feel that you've failed. Pull out your list and remind yourself why you want to quit. If your reasons have changed, make a new list.

Watch for "smoke signals"—like a friend lighting up. Know that this is the time when you're most likely to smoke. Be strong. It will pay off.

Chapter **11**

Finding Help

It is very hard to quit smoking. If you need help, don't be afraid to ask for it. There are many organizations that are ready to help.

The American Cancer Society has a program called "Smoking Cessation Clinics for High School Students." The program is made up of nine one-hour sessions. The Cancer Society trains someone from your school, the school nurse or a teacher. That person runs the clinic.

Check with your principal, school nurse, or guidance counselor to find out if your school offers this program. If the school doesn't have the program, you can help get one started. Look up

the American Cancer Society in your local phone
book. Or write to:

American Cancer Society
261 Madison Avenue
New York, NY 10016

The American Lung Association and the
American Heart Association are two other
organizations that are ready to help. They each
have many stop-smoking programs. Write to:

American Lung Association
1740 Broadway
New York, NY 10019

American Heart Association
7320 Greenville Avenue
Dallas, TX 75231

Quitting smoking is always a positive step. No
matter how long you have smoked, your body will
recover from at least some of the bad effects once
you stop.

If someone you know has tried to quit and failed,
maybe a doctor can help. There are drugs now
available to help those who can't seem to quit.
Some people have been helped by a chewing gum
that a doctor can prescribe. And some people have
been helped by wearing patches on their skin. The
patches release nicotine into the bodies of people
who wear them. The chewing gum also provides
the body with nicotine. These people cannot break
their addiction to nicotine. But at least their lungs—
and the lungs of those around them—are no longer
in danger.

Glossary—*Explaining New Words*

addictive   Causing a person's body to depend on a chemical.

adrenal gland   Produces the hormone adrenaline. Adrenaline prepares the body for emergency action. It makes the heart work harder.

bronchi   Tubes in the lungs.

cancer   A disease that causes cells to grow abnormally and become tumors. These tumors spread and interfere with normal cell growth.

carbon dioxide   A gas that is breathed out of the body when exhaling.

carbon monoxide   A gas that is poisonous. It is one of the chemicals in cigarette smoke.

chronic bronchitis   A lung condition caused by smoking. It is marked by severe coughing and irritation of the lungs.

cilia Tiny hairs in the bronchi that clear away mucus.

craving A great desire or longing.

drag A slang term for inhaling cigarette smoke.

emphysema A severe lung disease.

glamorous Full of excitement and romance.

heart disease There are many different diseases, including heart attack, stroke, hardening of the arteries, and blood clots.

influence To sway or affect.

mainstream smoke What the smoker inhales.

mucus A slippery secretion of the mucous membranes.

nicotine A drug found in tobacco smoke that your body becomes addicted to.

passive smoking Being affected by the smoking of others.

peer pressure A feeling that you should do something because others do it, or want you to do it.

premature (birth) Early, before fully ready.

sidestream smoke The smoke that comes from the burning end of a cigarette.

stress Tension or pressure.

tar A sticky, black substance found in tobacco. It coats the lungs when smoke is inhaled.

withdrawal Process of stopping the body's dependency on an addictive drug. Physical and mental effects an addict suffers after ceasing to take an addictive drug.

For Further Reading

Casey, Harry F. "A Sure Way to Stop Smoking."
Reader's Digest (Canadian). September 1986,
pages 71–74. This article gives a scary
description of lung cancer.

Goode, Erika F. "A New Addictive Drug:
Nicotine." *U.S. News & World Report.* May 30,
1988, pages 63–64. This article discusses the
effects of nicotine on the body.

Krogh, David. *Smoking, The Artificial Passion.* New
York: W.H. Freeman & Co., 1991. This book
for young people is a history of smoking, which
includes a chapter on how to quit smoking.

Malanka, Phyllis A. "Why Do We Smoke?"
Health. February, 1986, pages 32–35. This
article discusses why people might start smoking.
It also discusses specific health risks to smokers.

Robinson, Mary. *Giving It Up Mom.* New York:
Houghton Mifflin, 1989. This book is fiction,
but its message is real. Kids can help their
parents to quit smoking.

Teltsch, Kathleen. "Keeping Teen-Agers
Smokeless." *The New York Times*, August 18,
1992, pages B1, B4. A town in New Jersey
works hard to keep teens from smoking.

Index

About the Author

Elizabeth Keyishian is an Associate Editor for an award-winning children's science magazine. In addition to writing for young adults, she has published humorous essays (most recently in *Glamour* Magazine.) A graduate of Wesleyan University, Ms. Keyishian lives in New York City.

About the Editor

Evan Stark is a well-known sociologist, educator, and therapist as well as a popular lecturer on women's and children's health issues. Dr. Stark was the Henry Rutgers Fellow at Rutgers University, an associate at the Institution for Social and Policy Studies at Yale University, and a Fulbright Fellow at the University of Essex. He is the author of many publications in the field of family relations and is the father of four children.

Acknowledgments and Photo Credits

P. 11 H. Armstrong Roberts, Inc.; all other photos, Stuart Rabinowitz

Design/Production: Blackbirch Graphics, Inc.
Cover Photograph: Stuart Rabinowitz

WATERLOO HIGH SCHOOL LIBRARY
1464 INDUSTRY RD.
ATWATER, OHIO 44201

Everything you need to know about sm   16398
Keyishian, Elizabeth   613.85 Key